WAI'ANAE DIET COOKBOOK *'ELUA*

Volume II

A Companion Volume to
"The Wai'anae Book of Hawaiian Health"
and
"The Wai'anae Diet Cookbook"

This book is dedicated in memory of Dr. Frances Sydow of Kahumana Farm, whose vision and foresight prepared a place for the Wai'anae Diet Program to grow.

AN INVITATION

We invite you to participate in a great movement to restore the health of the people of *Hawai'i*. Right now, it is not the number of people involved that is important, but your depth of commitment. We believe that when enough individuals make a commitment to create their own *lōkahi*, health will follow. And when enough *kānaka maoli* are *lōkahi* within themselves . . . with others . . . with the land . . . with the food they eat . . . then the health of the people will be restored, and the birthrights of the *kānaka maoli* will follow.

Proceeds from the sale of this book will be used for the promotion of the *Wai'anae* Diet Program.

No Ka Wai'anae Diet
Haku 'ia na Mililani Allen
March 16, 1992

E Kūkulu kumuhana nā po'e Hawai'i
Pull together Hawaiian people

Hemolele i ka hihia
Free the entanglements

Ho'okuakahi i ka pōhaku
Clear the way of stones

E 'ai i ke kalo
Eat the taro

Ke kino o Hāloa
The body of Hāloa

E inu i ka wai
Drink the water

Ka wai ola o Kāne
The waters of life of Kāne

E kūkulu kumuhana nā po'e Hawai'i
Pull together Hawaiian people

Ho'ola ke kino
Heal the body

Hui 'ia mākou i ka ola kino.
We join together in health.

Editors

Helen Kanawaliwali O'Connor, C.H.W., Health Educator
Rozalyn Kalei'aukai Teixeira, Health Educator
Monica Tan, R.D.
Sheila Beckham, R.D., M.P.H., C.D.E.
Terry Shintani, J.D., M.D., M.P.H.

Cover Art

Ka Pu'uwai O Ka Po'e, "The Heart of the People," by Kawena Young

Illustrations

Helen Kanawaliwali O'Connor, C.H.W., Health Educator
Eric Enos
Eric Uptegrove
Rozalyn Kalei'aukai Teixeira, Health Educator

Desktop Publishing

Jan Foster

TABLE OF CONTENTS

ACKNOWLEDGMENT . . . . *xi*
PREFACE . . . . *xiii*
INTRODUCTION
   About the *Wai'anae* Diet Program *1*
Lā'ī *3*
   Deboning *Lā'ī* *3*
   Preparing *Lāwalu* *5*
PRINCIPAL FOODS OF THE *WAI'ANAE* DIET *7*
   Kalo *9*
      Mo'olelo O Hāloa *10*
      'Oha *11*
      Lau Kalo *12*
      Hāhā *13*
         Steamed *Kalo* *14*
         Boiled *Kalo* *14*
         Poi *15*
         Stuffed *Kalo* *16*
         Kalo Stuffing *16*
         Kalo Fish Cakes *17*
         Kalo Bean Salad *17*
         Kalo Muffins *18*
         Pa'i'ai Wai'ū *18*
         Kalo Pudding *19*
         Kalo Pie *19*
         Kalo Cake *20*

Kalo (continued)

- *Lau Kalo* 21
- Chicken *Lāwalu* 21
- Chicken *Lūʻau* 22
- *Hāhā* (Vegetable) 22
- Chicken *Hāhā* 23
- *Hāhā* Stir Fry 23

ʻUala 24
- *Moʻolelo O ʻUala* 25
- Steamed *ʻUala* 26
- *Lau ʻUala* (Vegetable) 26
- Chicken With *ʻUala* and *Maiʻa* 27
- *ʻUala* Chicken Casserole 28
- *Lau ʻUala* Salad 28
- *ʻUala*, *Kalo* and Fruit Salad 29
- *ʻUala* Pudding 29

ʻUlu 31
- Steamed *ʻUlu* 32
- Baked *ʻUlu* 32
- *ʻUlu* Poi 33
- *ʻUlu* Hekka 33
- *ʻUlu* With Mushrooms and *Hōʻiʻo* 34
- Herb *ʻUlu* Salad 35
- *ʻUlu* Salad 36

OTHER FOODS OF THE *WAIʻANAE* DIET 37

Seafood 38
- *Ka ʻŌpelu* 39
- How to Prepare *ʻŌpelu* 39
- Raw *ʻŌpelu* 40
- *ʻŌpelu Kupa* 40

Seafood (continued)

ʻĀweoweo Kai	41
Kala	41
Halalū	42
Manini	42
Pakaliao	43
Pakaliao Kū	43
Poke	43
Poke Iʻa	44
Limu Kohu Poke	44
Poke Shoyu Style	44
Pipipi	45
Pipipi Kupa	45
Kūpeʻe	46
Kūpeʻe and Black Beans	46
Hōʻonoʻono ʻAi	47
Paʻakai	47
ʻAlaea	48
Kai Nīʻoi	49
ʻInamona	49
Limu	50
Moʻolelo O Nā Limu	51
Limu Līpeʻepeʻe Salad	52
Limu Wāwaeʻiole Salad	52
Limu ʻEleʻEle	53
Ferns	54
Hōʻiʻo	54
Preparing Hōʻiʻo	55
Hōʻiʻo Salad	55
Hāpuʻu	56
How to Prepare Hāpuʻu Shoots	57

Ferns (continued)

- *Hāpu'u* Hekka 57
- **Fruits Used on the *Wai'anae* Diet** 59
  - *Mai'a* 60
  - *'Alani* 60
  - *Mīkana* 61
  - *Hala Kahiki* 61
    - Frozen *Mai'a* Dessert 62
    - Mixed Fruit Salad 62
- **Other Fruits of *Hawai'i*** 63
  - *'Ōhelo* Berries 64
  - *Kuawa* 64
  - *Manakō* 64
  - *'Ōhi'a 'Ai* 65
  - *Liliko'i* 65
  - *Pohā* 65
    - Fruit Relish 66
    - *Wai Hua* 66
    - *Manakō* Smoothie 67
    - *'Ōhelo 'Alani* Jam 67
- **Hawaiian Herb Teas** 68
  - *Ko'oko'olau* 68
  - *Wāpine* 69
  - *Mamaki* 69
    - Hot Tea 70
    - Iced Tea 70
- **GLOSSARY** 71

ACKNOWLEDGMENT

The *Wai'anae* Diet Program would like to express our fondest *mahalo nui* to the Office of Hawaiian Affairs (OHA) for their generosity in the development of this book. We are fortunate for their firm belief in all that the *Wai'anae* Diet stands for. Through their assistance, we have been able to provide the information needed to help the people of *Hawai'i* choose a healthier lifestyle . . . a lifestyle once lost.

'O mākou nō me ka ho'omaika'i,
Wai'anae Diet Mā

PREFACE

Cookbook *'Elua* was designed to share information and recipes on the traditional foods of *Hawai'i*. The recipes provided in this book reflect those used in the three-week *Wai'anae* Diet Program. They consist of traditional foods of *ka po'e Hawai'i* that have been handed down throughout the generations. While most are from *ka po'e Hawai'i*, some have been borrowed from other ethnic groups who have come to *Hawai'i* and become *'ohana* through their intermarriage with *ka po'e Hawai'i*.

We have included information on caloric content, grams of fat, and percent of fat for each recipe. The *Wai'anae* Diet's philosophy emphasizes a diet high in bulk to satisfy hunger and low in fat. It does not emphasize calorie counting.

Diets high in fat are risk factors for diabetes, heart disease, obesity, gall bladder disease, cancer, and arthritis. These conditions were virtually nonexistent in *Hawai'i* before westernization. The pre-Western contact diets in *Hawai'i* were approximately 10% fat. Risk increases when TOTAL DAILY FAT is elevated.

Daily fat intake may be made up of a combination of low and moderate fat items. Items such as seafood or poultry contain only protein and fat, therefore, will contain a higher percentage of fat compared to vegetable or starch dishes. Fat has 9 kcal per gram, so any item containing animal fat will have more calories coming from fat. To reduce obesity-related chronic disease risk, it is recommended that total fat consumption be limited.

Also included in this cookbook is a glossary. We hope that you will learn a little of the language as well as the foods of *ka poʻe Hawaiʻi*. There are *"moʻolelo liʻiliʻi"* for you to read along the way that tell not only of the foods, but a little of the lifestyle of a people whose language and culture are returning for a future that is stronger and brighter than ever.

Waiʻanae Diet Mā

INTRODUCTION

About the Waiʻanae Diet Program

The *Waiʻanae* Diet Cookbooks are designed as companion volumes to the *Waiʻanae* Book of Hawaiian Health for anyone to use so that he or she may reap the benefits of a healthy diet modeled after the traditional Hawaiian diet as presented in the *Waiʻanae* Diet Program. As a central focus, the *Waiʻanae* Diet Program was designed as a culturally-appropriate, community-based intervention program with special consideration to accessibility, reasonable cost, and ability to be propagated and sustained in the community. The program was designed primarily to deal with the disproportionately high rates of obesity, disease, and mortality among the *kānaka maoli* population at the Waianae Coast Comprehensive Health Center where 52% of its patients are of *kānaka maoli* descent.

The program is based on groups of participants who follow three-week periods of the strict traditional diet of the *kānaka maoli* with close medical monitoring. Education sessions include cultural teachings, and sessions covering spiritual, mental, emotional, and physical health. Participants are encouraged to become role models for others and thus impact on others. Follow-up sessions and "transition diet" classes are also designed for the participants to sustain the dietary changes encouraged in the diet program.

The initial selection of foods on the program consists of foods eaten in *Hawai'i* before Western influence such as *kalo*; *poi*; *'uala*; *uhi*; *'ulu*; greens such as *hō'i'o*, *lū'au*, *lau 'uala*, and *lau uhi*; fruit; *limu*; fish; and chicken.

All foods are served either raw or steamed in a manner that approximates ancient styles of cooking. The diet approximates that of *ka po'e kāhiko* which was estimated to contain less than 10% fat, 12% to 15% protein, and 75% to 78% carbohydrate. The program teaches not only the traditional diet of the *kānaka maoli*, but also a "transition diet" which provides food alternatives so that the program may be continued as a permanent part of one's lifestyle.

On the *Wai'anae* Diet Program protocol, participants generally lose weight and patients with diabetes also demonstrate improved blood sugar control. In addition, blood pressures have improved as well as other ailments such as arthritis, headaches, hypercholesterolemia, hyperlipidemia, and many other conditions. The results of the program has been published in the American Journal of Clinical Nutrition.[1]

---

[1] T.T. Shintani, C.K. Hughes, S. Beckham, H.K. O'Connor. Obesity and Cardiovascular Risk Intervention Through the "ad libitum" Feeding of Traditional Hawaiian Diet, Am J Clin Nutr 1991;53:1647S-51S.

LĀ'Ī

Before going on to the recipe portion of this book, we would like to give you some useful information about the *lā'ī*.

The *lā'ī* has many purposes. It is a strong leaf that is long, wide, smooth, odorless, and shiny. The *lā'ī* is used for ceremonial and religious purposes. Garments of plaited leaves, rain capes, sandals, and *hula* skirts were made from *lā'ī*. It is used to thatch roofs and sides of houses. It is wrapped around the head to relieve headaches, over the body to lower fever, used as bandages, and to purify menstruating women. *Lā'ī* is also used for protection to ward off evil thoughts or spirits. It is rare that you will find a home in *Hawai'i* that does not have *lā'ī* planted in the yard. The *lā'ī* can be tied and folded several ways to carry small amounts of food and is used to wrap food for cooking.

DEBONING *LĀ'Ī*

To use the *lā'ī* for *lawalu* or wrapping you need to remove the rib or bone, so that the stem becomes pliable for tying. Begin by picking a fresh green leaf. When picking *lā'ī* you should pick the leaves from the bottom of the plant first, leaving the top leaves. To strip the *lā'ī* off the plant, grab the stem of the *lā'ī* and pull down sharply, holding onto the stalk with the other hand.

To debone, wash your leaf first then turn the leaf with the shiny side facing down. Cut or bite the bone about one-third down from the top of the end of the stem. Cut or bite the bone without breaking through. To strip off the bone without making a *puka* in the *lā'ī*, hold your hand as illustrated below, separating the bone from the surface of the *lā'ī*.

Place *lā'ī* shiny side down

Stem

Make cut or bite about one-third from top of stem bone.

How to debone:

Press bone away from leaf and strip off with one motion.

PREPARING *LĀWALU**

Place the deboned *lā'ī* shiny side up. Place fish on top.

Place a 2nd *lā'ī* over, shiny side down, facing fish.

Take a 3rd *lā'ī* and curl around as pictured. Try to curl edges of 1st *lā'ī* so cooking juices stay inside of *lā'ī* when cooking.

Take a 4th *lā'ī* and curl around as pictured.

Take the loose ends of stems and tie each end.

This takes a little practice and the size of the *lā'ī* leaf is important, but if done properly you have a cooking package that is neat and efficient. When *pau*, you have a nice *lā'ī* platter to eat from.

---

* *Drawings and text by Eric Enos from "Hawaiian Style" published by the 'Ōpelu Project Inc., Wai'anae, Hawai'i.*

PRINCIPAL FOODS OF THE *WAI'ANAE* DIET

KALO

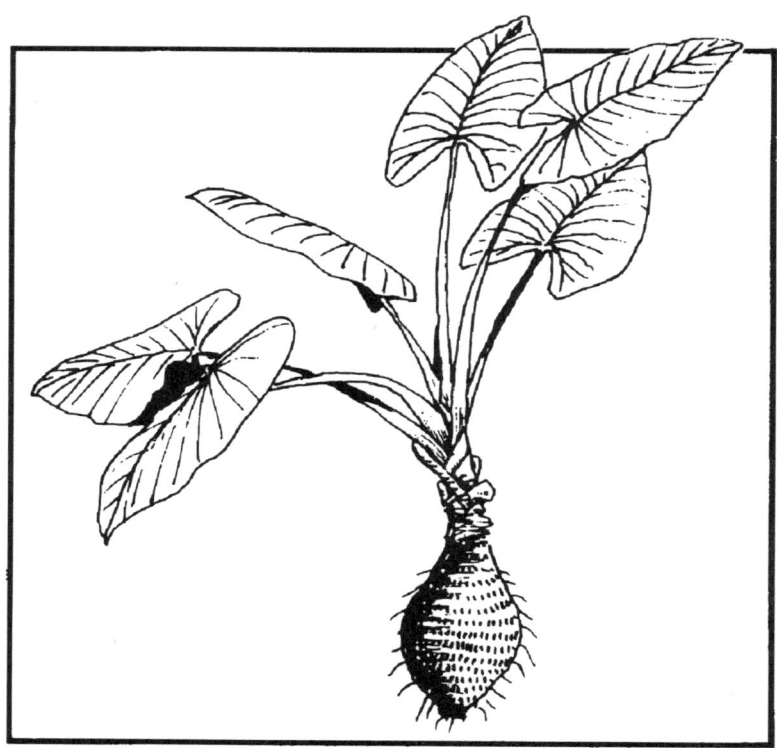

Kalo is the staff of life for the *kānaka maoli*. It has strong *mana* and had much to do with sustaining large populations of human beings over hundreds of years.

KALO

Kalo was brought to *Hawai'i* by the first Polynesians. The *kalo* plant is a very important food staple for the *kānaka maoli*.

Kalo has a high concentration of calcium oxalate, which are needle-like crystals found throughout the entire plant. *Kalo* must be cooked properly. If it is eaten raw or half cooked, it may cause itching in the throat.

Kalo, used to make *poi* or eaten whole, is the primary staple of the *kānaka maoli*. Every part of the *kalo* plant is used: the leaves, the stem, the flower, and the corm. The skin can be used for animal feed or fertilizer.

The *kānaka maoli* cultivated over 200 varieties of *kalo* for different purposes. Today only a few varieties remain.

Kalo is considered sacred by the *kānaka maoli*. In mythology of *Hawai'i*, *kalo*, the symbol of *Hāloanaka*, is considered the elder brother of the *kānaka maoli*.

Moʻolelo O Hāloa
(The Story of Hāloa)

Many years ago, when there were only the heavens and the earth, *Wākea* (sky father) kept watch over the heavens and Papa (earth mother) ruled the earth. Through the mating of *Wākea* with *Papa*, a *keiki* was conceived. This *keiki* was stillborn and put to the earth in the eastern corner where the sun shone first on each new day.

Soon a strange plant sprouted from the spot where the *keiki* had been buried. Its broad green leaves grew on long stalks that swayed in the breeze. They named this firstborn *keiki kāne* "Hāloanaka" because of its *naka* (quivering) leaves and *hāloa* (long) stems. The *kalo* continued to grow, producing many offshoots called *ʻoha*. These *keiki* were planted and more *ʻoha* were produced until the *kalo* was bountiful in *Hawaiʻi*.

Another child was later born and he was named "Hāloa" after his older brother. He had many *ʻoha* or children and his descendants are the *kānaka maoli*.

A strong bond holds the *kānaka maoli* to the *kalo*. *Ka poʻe kahiko* say that it was the will of God that *Hāloanaka* was born first, for he provided the necessary food for all those who came later.

In reverence to this older brother, the people of *Hawaiʻi* considered the *kalo* a sacred plant. *Nā wāhine* were not allowed to handle the *kalo* at all. When the *poi* bowl was placed on the table, the people were not allowed to argue or speak in anger while eating.

The *kalo* plant with its *ʻoha* is likened to a family with its *keiki*. Thus, the term *ʻohana* was used to include all members of the family.

'Oha

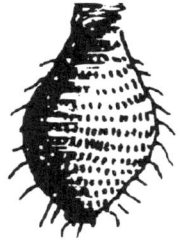

The *'oha* must be cooked properly. Do not peel the skin off the *kalo* prior to boiling or steaming. It is easier and less itchy to cook unpeeled and peel it after it is cooked.

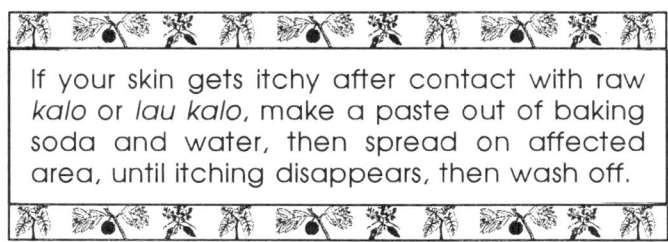

If your skin gets itchy after contact with raw *kalo* or *lau kalo*, make a paste out of baking soda and water, then spread on affected area, until itching disappears, then wash off.

Lau Kalo

The *lau kalo* are delicious when prepared properly. The *lau kalo* contain microscopic calcium oxalate crystals, which are like fine needles and must be broken down by cooking. *Lau kalo* that is not cooked well will cause an unpleasant itchiness in the throat when eaten.

The *lau kalo* is very high in calcium, iron, and vitamins. It is one of the most nutritious foods of *Hawai'i*.

Tip on Preventing Itchiness When Cleaning *Lau Kalo*

If you travel through various areas in *Hawai'i*, you will find different methods to prevent itchiness when preparing the *lau kalo*.

The most common method is to pinch off the three tips of the *lau kalo*. The *hāhā* and the underside of the *lau kalo* are then peeled at the *piko*, prior to cooking. The oxalate crystals can then be released during cooking to flow through the open ends of the *lau kalo*.

Hāhā

Hāhā is the stem of the *kalo* plant. Like the other parts of this plant it is delicious cooked by itself, or with other foods. It should NOT be eaten raw. To use, take the *hāhā* from the *lau kalo*, peel off the outer skin, and rinse.

 ## STEAMED *KALO*

Wash/scrub *kalo* until clean. Place whole *kalo* in a steamer or pressure cooker with water. Steam on high for 2 hours (or in a pressure cooker for 1 hour). The *kalo* is fully cooked when fork tender. Cool under cold tap water. Remove outer skin by scraping with a dull knife or spoon. Cut into slices or cubes. Serve warm or cold. *(½ cup = 93.5 kcal., 0.075 gm. fat, 0.7% fat)*

 ## BOILED *KALO*

1-2 lbs. *Kalo*
Water

Scrub *kalo* thoroughly, then place in a large pot. Add water to half cover the *kalo*. Cover pot and boil 2 hours or until fork tender. Peel *kalo* when cooled and slice or cube. Serve warm or cold. *(½ cup = 93.5 kcal., 0.075 gm. fat, 0.7% fat)*

Papa kuʻi ʻai with *pōhaku kuʻi ʻai*

The recipe for making *poi* we share in this cookbook is a fast and simple way to prepare *poi* for today's lifestyle. The original way of preparing *poi* can take hours. First the *kalo* was picked from the *lo'i*. It was then cooked in the *imu*. Later, it was cleaned, cut into pieces, and pounded on a *papa ku'i 'ai* with a *pōkahu ku'i 'ai*, made and shaped out of special *pōhaku*. This process made *pa'i'ai*. When *pa'i'ai* was made, it was enough for two days, up to 500 pounds. This *pa'i'ai* was mixed with water to make what is known as *poi*. The Wai'anae Book of Hawaiian Health, 1993, has a picture of pounding poi on page 16.

 *Poi*

Cut cooked and peeled *kalo* into 4" to 6" rectangles and blend to a smooth pudding like consistency in a blender, or food processor, while the *kalo* is still slightly warm. After *kalo* has been processed and cooled, add water and mix until you have a desired consistency.

- Some people prefer a heavier consistency, which is the one-finger *poi*. Very little water has been added to this type.

- A thinner version is the two-finger *poi*, which has more water.

- An even thinner type is the three-finger *poi* that is very hard to pick up.

In *Hawai'i* all visitors are welcomed into the home. It is said that one could tell the generosity of the host by the thickness of the *poi* offered to you. One finger meant a generous host, two was acceptable, but three-finger *poi* was the sign of a stingy person.

STUFFED *KALO*

6 lbs.	*Kalo* (approximately 6 medium)
3 cloves	Garlic
1	Round onion, diced
1	Bell pepper, diced
	Pa'akai to taste

Scoop out meat from center of *kalo*, leaving sides thick enough to remain firm when stuffed. Mash scooped *kalo*. Saute garlic, onions and bell peppers in frying pan sprayed with Pam. Add mashed *kalo* and *pa'akai* and mix well. Stuff into *kalo* casing. Bake in oven at 350° F. until tops are brown. Cut lengthwise. Makes 12 servings.
(1 serving = 328 kcal., 0.278 gm. fat, 0.9% fat)

KALO STUFFING

6 cups	Wheat bread, toasted and cubed
3 cups	*Kalo*, cooked and diced
2 large	Round onions, finely chopped
3 stalks	Celery, diced
3 tsp.	Dried parsley
2 tsp.	Sage
2 tsp.	Thyme
1 tsp.	Savory
1 tsp.	Marjoram
1 tsp.	Garlic powder
1 tsp.	*Pa'akai*
12 oz.	Chicken broth
1 pkg.	Shiitake mushroom (8 oz.)

Cook all ingredients together except for bread crumbs and *kalo*. Cook for 15 minutes. Add *kalo* and cook 5 minutes longer. (continued next page)

Toss with bread cubes using a fork. Stir in chicken broth slowly to desired consistency. Makes 12, 1 cup servings. *(1 cup = 462 kcal., 5.685 gm. fat, 11% fat)*

 ## KALO FISH CAKES

2 cups	*Kalo*, cooked and mashed
2 Tbsp.	Round onion, grated
1 cup	Fish, raw and scraped
	Pa'akai for taste

Mix onion and fish to mashed *kalo*. Mix well. Form into 3" round cakes and pan fry in a non-stick skillet until golden brown (may use Pam). Makes 12 to 15 fish cakes. *(1 serving = 54.6 kcal., 0.536 gm. fat, 8.8% fat)*

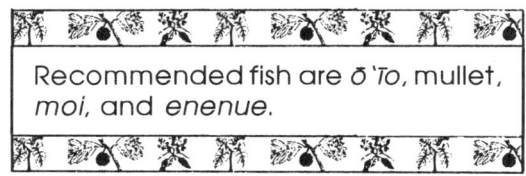

Recommended fish are *ō'io*, mullet, *moi*, and *enenue*.

KALO BEAN SALAD

2 cups	*Kalo*, cooked and diced
1 med.	Round onions, chopped
1 med.	Red bell pepper, chopped julienne style
1 large	Green bell pepper, chopped
1 can	Kidney beans (15 oz.), drain/rinse
1 cup	No-oil Italian dressing
1 can	Garbanzo beans (15 oz.)
1 can	Wax beans (15 oz.)

Mix all ingredients together, chill and serve. Makes 8, 1 cup servings. *(1 cup = 159 kcal., 2.5 gm. fat, 14% fat)*

 ## *KALO* MUFFINS

2 cups	Whole wheat flour
2 Tbsp.	Sugar
2 tsp.	Baking powder
½ tsp.	*Pa'akai*
1 cup	*Kalo*, cooked and mashed
1¼ cups	Skim milk
2	Egg whites, beaten

In a large bowl combine flour, sugar, baking powder and salt; mix in *kalo*. Combine milk and eggs. Stir into *kalo* mixture until lightly blended. Pour into paper-lined muffin pan. Bake 25 to 30 minutes at 325° F. or until a food pick inserted in center comes out clean.

 ## *PA'I'AI WAI'Ū*

½ cup	*Pa'i'ai*
½ cup	Skim milk, warm

Place *pa'i'ai* in a cereal bowl. Add warm skim milk.
(1 serving = 177 kcal., 0.391 gm. fat, 2% fat)

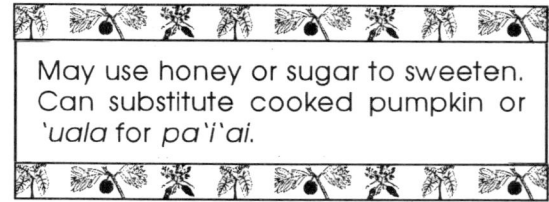

May use honey or sugar to sweeten. Can substitute cooked pumpkin or *'uala* for *pa'i'ai*.

Kalo Pudding

2 cups	*Kalo*, cooked and mashed
2	Egg whites, slightly beaten
3 Tbsp.	Water
3 Tbsp.	Brown sugar

Mix taro with water, egg and brown sugar. Batter will be thick. Spread into greased 8" pan sprayed with Pam and bake in preheated oven at 350° F. for 1 hour. Makes 4, ½ cup servings. *(1 serving = 140.8 kcal., 0.075 gm. fat, 0.479% fat)*

Kalo Pie

3½ cups	*Pa'i'ai*
2 cups	Coconut water
1 tsp.	Cornstarch
¼ cup	Raw sugar cane juice *or*
	1/3 cup raw brown sugar
½ cup	Young coconut *or* dehydrated coconut flakes

Place *kalo* and add *poi* into a blender or food processor. Slowly add coconut water, cornstarch, sugar cane juice, and coconut. Blend to smooth consistency. Pour into uncooked pie shell and bake in preheated oven at 300° F. for 1 hour. Makes 8 servings. *(1 serving <u>not including pie shell</u> = 217 kcal., 4.274 gm. fat, 18% fat)*

Kalo Cake

1 cup	Whole wheat flour
½ cup	White flour
½ tsp.	Baking soda
3/4 tsp.	Cinnamon
½ cup	Sugar
1 cup	*Poi*
¼ cup	Applesauce
½ tsp.	Vanilla extract
2	Egg whites
½ cup	*Kalo*, chopped (optional)

Preheat oven to 350° F. Lightly coat a loaf pan with baking spray. In a large bowl, sift together the whole wheat flour, white flour, baking soda, cinnamon, and half of the sugar. Set aside.

In a small bowl, mix together the *poi*, applesauce, and vanilla extract. Set aside.

In a separate bowl, beat the egg whites until they hold stiff peaks. Slowly add the remaining sugars and beat until the whites hold glossy peaks.

Combine the *poi* mixture with the flour mixture. (Fold in optional chopped *kalo* at this time.) Carefully fold the egg whites into this mixture until no white streaks show in the batter. Pour into loaf pan and bake for 45 minutes or until a toothpick inserted comes out clean. Makes 8 servings.
(1 serving without added kalo = 223.3 kcal., 0.429 gm. fat, 1.7% fat) (1 serving with added kalo = 246 kcal., 0.448 gm. fat, 1.6% fat)

LAU KALO

1 lb.	*Lau kalo*
2 qts.	Water

Boil 2 quarts of water and add cleaned *lau kalo*. The *hāhā* may also be added or saved for later use. When all the *lau kalo* has been added and wilted down, bring to a full boil, then turn heat to medium and let simmer for ½ hour to 1 hour. (Cooking time is shorter if *hahā* is cooked separately.) Strain cooked *lau kalo* in colander then rinse in cold water. Serve hot or cool.

Cooled *lū'au* may be bagged for freezing.

CHICKEN LĀWALU

5 - 7	*Lau kalo*
2 oz.	Chicken, skinless, boneless
Pinch	*Pa'akai* (optional)
2 med.	*Lā'ī* (deboned)

Cut stems from *lau kalo* and wash thoroughly. Stack 5 to 7 *lau kalo* leaves on each other. Place chicken in center of leaves and sprinkle pinch of *pa'akai* (optional) and wrap *lau kalo* to cover the chicken. Wrap in *lā'ī* and steam in a covered container for approximately 2 hours. See page 5 for wrapping illustrations. Serve hot. Makes 1 serving.

(1 serving = 76 kcal., 1.5 gm. fat, 18% fat)

CHICKEN *LŪʻAU*

2 lbs.	Chicken, skinless, boneless
1 Tbsp.	Crushed ginger
4 lbs.	*Lūʻau*
2 qts.	Water
	Paʻakai to taste

Cut chicken into bite-size pieces then saute with ginger in a large pot sprayed with Pam. Add water and bring to a boil. Lower heat and simmer for ½ hour or until chicken is tender. Stir in *lūʻau* and *paʻakai* to taste. Simmer on low heat for ½ hour, stirring occasionally. Serve hot. Makes 12, 1 cup servings. *(1 cup = 148 kcal., 2 gm. fat, 13% fat)*

HĀHĀ (Vegetable)

1 lb.	*Hāhā*, cleaned
	Water
	Paʻakai to taste

Wash and peel *hāhā* stems. Cut into 1" pieces. Cover with water and bring to a boil. Partially cover pot until *hāhā* begins to wilt, then simmer for 10 minutes; drain. Add *paʻakai* to taste. (Check for itchiness.) Serve hot or cold. Makes 4 servings. *(1 serving = 33 kcal., 0.228 gm. fat, 6.2% fat)*

Chicken *Hāhā*

2 lbs.	*Hāhā*, cut in 2" to 3" pieces
2 lbs.	Chicken, skinless, boneless, cubed
1 med.	Round onion, diced
1 clove	Garlic, medium size and grated
	Pa'akai for taste

In 2 cups boiling water, simmer *hāhā* for 15 to 20 minutes, or until wilted. Brown chicken with onions and garlic, in a skillet with Pam. Add drained *hāhā* and simmer for 30 minutes. Makes 4 servings. *(1 serving = 366 kcal., 6.6 gm. fat, 16.2% fat)*

Hāhā Stir Fry

1 lb.	*He'e or* calamari
1	Round onion, cut julienne style
1	Tomato, cut into wedges
1	Bell pepper, cut julienne style
1 Tbsp.	Braggs amino acids
1 cup	*Hāhā*, cleaned and cut into 1" pieces

Heat wok and spray with Pam. Clean and slice *he'e* into thin strips. Add *hāhā* and cook about 10 minutes. Add the balance of the vegetables and stir for 8 to 10 minutes. Serve hot. (May add *nī'oi* if desired.) Makes 4 servings. *1 serving = 150 kcal., 2 gm. fat, 12% fat*

'UALA

It is known from written history that early Polynesians brought the *'uala* to *Hawai'i*. *'Uala* is a vine that sprawls close to the ground and produces tubers along the stems under the ground.

The tuber or root of the sweet potato was the second most important food staple for the *kānaka maoli*. The tubers were baked in the *imu* and eaten or baked and mashed to make *poi*. The tubers were also grated and mixed with coconut milk, wrapped in *lā'ī* and baked for dessert. The young leaves of the plant were cooked and used as vegetables.

There were said to be 230 varieties of *lau 'uala* in ancient times, but today, only 24 varieties remain.

Moʻolelo O ʻUala

The *ʻuala* is just one of the many *kino lau* of the demigod *Kamapuaʻa*. *ʻUala* grows in dirt mounds, symbolizing mounds that pigs dig up in the earth. This particular trait is spoken of in the *"Kumulipo"* (creation chant) during the fifth period of *Pō*:

> "His snout was of great size and with it (he) dug the earth, he dug until he raised a great mound, . . ."

Sometimes these mounds refer to the descendants of *Kamapuaʻa*. These mounds can also represent burial grounds, reminding us of the generations that came before.

The leaf of the *ʻuala* plant has three points like that of a pig; the two ears and the snout. The *ʻuala* itself resembles the excrement of the pig.

The state fish, *Humuhumunukunukuapuaʻa*, is another form of *Kamapuaʻa* which he used to escape his would be captors. The skin of this fish is very tough like that of a boar. Should you dive underwater and be lucky enough to hear the *humuhumunukunukuapuaʻa*, you will notice that it makes sounds like that of a pig.

 ## STEAMED ʻUALA

Wash *ʻuala* and pour about 3/4" to 1" of water into a pot or steamer. Place *ʻuala* on the steamer rack and cover. Steam for 25 to 30 minutes or until fork tender.
(4 oz. serving = 116 kcal., 0.124 gm.fat, 0.9% fat)

> If you have a rice cooker, place enough water in the bottom to cover the first joint of your index finger and place the *ʻuala* on the rack. Turn on the rice cooker and when it turns itself off, the *ʻuala* should be done.

 ## LAU ʻUALA (Vegetable)

| 1 lb. | Young *lau ʻuala* |
| | Water |

One trick to having delicious *ʻuala* greens to eat is to pick the young tender shoots. Take a large handful of young leaves and place into boiling water for approximately 5 minutes. Drain the leaves in a colander, place in a bowl, and add seasoning to taste. Makes 4, 4 oz. servings.

> Add chopped tomatoes and onions and the juice of a lemon to make a refreshing salad. Or add cooked chicken, *ʻōpae*, etc. to make a delicious meal.

CHICKEN WITH *'UALA* AND *MAI'A*

---

2 lbs.	Chicken, remove skin and cut into pieces
½ cup	Round onions, chopped
1 clove	Garlic, crushed
2 Tbsp.	Whole wheat flour
1 tsp.	*Pa'akai*
¼ tsp.	Black pepper
1	Bay leaf
1 cup	Chicken broth *or* 1 chicken bouillon cube dissolved in 1 cup boiling water
1 can	Tomatoes (8 oz.), drained
2 large	*'Uala*, peeled and cut in 1½" slices
4	*Mai'a*, peeled and halved

Saute chicken in skillet with Pam until well browned. Remove from skillet and pour off drippings. Saute onion and garlic about 3 minutes, or until soft. Stir in flour, salt, and pepper. Add bay leaf, chicken stock, and tomatoes. Mix well. Add 3/4 cup water. Return chicken to skillet. Add *'uala*. Cover and simmer 45 minutes.

In another skillet, saute *mai'a* in Pam until golden. When ready to serve, place chicken and *'uala* on platter and surround with *mai'a*. Makes 8, 1 cup servings.
(1 cup = 336 kcal., 8.7 gm. fat, 23% fat)

'UALA CHICKEN CASSEROLE

2 lbs.	Chicken, skinless, boneless
3 lbs.	*'Uala*, cooked and mashed
1 lb.	*Lau 'uala*
1 large	Round onion, sliced
2 cloves	Garlic, medium size and diced
	Pam cooking spray *or* ¼ cup water
1 tsp.	*Pa'akai*

Cut chicken into 1" or 2" pieces. Saute in Pam or ¼ cup of water. Add garlic and onions. Lower heat and simmer until cooked. Parboil *lau 'uala* for 3 minutes. Mash *'uala*. Lay chicken pieces, *lau 'uala*, and mashed *'uala* in a pan sprayed with Pam. Bake for 15 to 20 minutes at 350° F. until the top browns. Makes 12, ½ cup servings.
(½ cup = 303 kcal., 9.313 gm. fat, 26.7% fat)

When a serving of this dish is eaten together with large amounts of principal foods and vegetables, as the Wai'anae Diet Program recommends, the <u>overall</u> diet can remain close to 10% fat.

LAU 'UALA SALAD

2 bunches	*Lau 'uala*
5 med.	Tomatoes, diced
3 med.	Round onions, diced
2 large	Lemons

Remove *lau 'uala* from the stem. Rinse well and place in a large bowl. Cover with hot boiling water to blanche.

(continued next page)

Pour contents into a colander and rinse under cold tap water to cool. In a large bowl, add tomatoes and onions to blanched leaves and toss. Sprinkle with lemon juice. Chill before serving. Serve cold. Makes 4, ½ cup servings. *(½ cup = 54 kcal., 0.454 gm. fat, 7.5% fat)*

'UALA, KALO AND FRUIT SALAD

½ cup	*Hala Kahiki*, cubed or balled
½ cup	*Mīkana*, cubed or balled
½ cup	*Mai'a*, sliced
½ cup	Melon, cubed or balled
½ cup	*'Uala* (cooked), cubed or balled
½ cup	*Kalo* (cooked), cubed or balled
2 cups	Plain non-fat yogurt

Toss all ingredients together and chill. Makes 6 to 8, ½ cup servings. *(½ cup = 117.4 kcal, 0.341 gm. fat, 2.6% fat)*

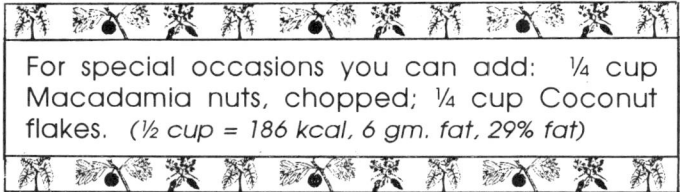

For special occasions you can add: ¼ cup Macadamia nuts, chopped; ¼ cup Coconut flakes. *(½ cup = 186 kcal, 6 gm. fat, 29% fat)*

'UALA PUDDING

2 cups	*'Uala*, cooked and mashed
2	Egg whites, slightly beaten
3 Tbsp.	Water
3 Tbsp.	Brown sugar

Mix *'uala* with water, eggs, and brown sugar. Batter will be thick. Spread into an 8" pan which has been sprayed with Pam and bake at 350° F. for 1 hour. Makes 4, ½ cup servings. *(½ cup = 219.3 kcal., 0.435 gm. fat, 2% fat)*

ʻUlu

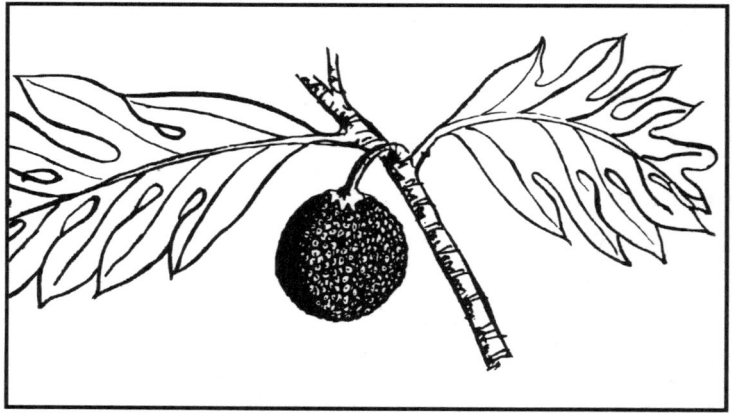

In a *moʻolelo* of *Hawaiʻi*, the god *Kū* saved his family during a famine when he planted himself into the ground and sprouted into a tree.

'ULU

'Ulu was brought to *Hawai'i* by early Polynesians and became a minor staple for the *kānaka maoli*.

Green *'ulu* is firm and slightly sweet and is eaten as a starch. The ripe *'ulu* is soft and yellowish green and is very sweet.

After picking, a milky white sap may bleed from the stem. Leave *'ulu* on heavy paper and let it bleed until the sap on the stem dries. It can then be prepared for cooking. (The sap from the *'ulu* will stain hands and clothing.)

The *lā'au 'ulu* has many uses. The young flower produces a tan dye; the old flowers a brown dye. The *kānaka maoli* used the sap as glue for joining gourds and caulking to fill the seams of the canoe. The trunk was used to make drums; *poi* boards; woodwork, canoe bows, and stern pieces.

 ## STEAMED ʻULU

    1 large   *ʻUlu*
                  Water

Wash *ʻulu*, cut in half or leave whole. Place in a steamer, with water. Steam on high heat for 1 hour. *ʻUlu* is fully cooked when fork tender. Cool under cold tap water and scrape off outer skin with a dull knife or a spoon. Cut into slices or cubes. Serve warm or cold.
(4 oz. serving = 102 kcal., 0.569 gm. fat)

 ## BAKED ʻULU

    1 large   *ʻUlu*
                  Water

Wash *ʻulu* and place in a baking dish with ½" water and bake for 1 hour at 350° F. *ʻUlu* is cooked when a bamboo skewer goes through easily and is clean when pulled out. Remove from oven and let cool. Twist off stem, core, and peel *ʻulu*. Slice into bite-size pieces. *(4 oz. serving = 102 kcal., 0.569 gm. fat)*

 ## ʻULU POI

    1 large   Ripe *ʻulu* (not too soft)
                 Water

Wash *ʻulu*, place in a pot and cover with water. Boil for 1 hour or until fork tender. Drain and cool. Scrape the skin and cut into slices. Pound *ʻulu* with a *pōhaku kuʻi ʻai* or grind in a master juicer or meat grinder. Place mixture in a large bowl and continue to mash the *ʻulu* with your hands, turning over each time, until smooth and thick. Mix in small amounts of water until you have the consistency you desire. Serve immediately or cover with ¼" water at the top, and refrigerate.

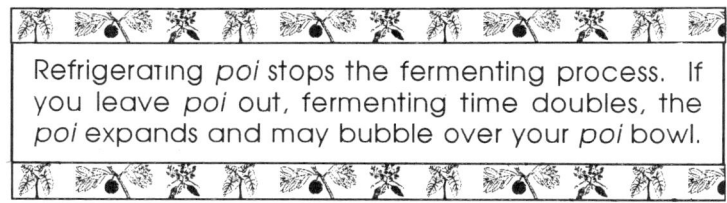

Refrigerating *poi* stops the fermenting process. If you leave *poi* out, fermenting time doubles, the *poi* expands and may bubble over your *poi* bowl.

ʻULU HEKKA

    1½ lbs.   Chicken, skinless and boneless
    3 lbs.   *ʻUlu*, cooked
    1 large   Round onion, sliced
    2 cloves Garlic, medium-size and diced
    1 bunch Green onions
                  Pam cooking spray *or* ½ cup water

Cut chicken into 1" to 2" pieces. Pan fry garlic and onions in Pam or ¼ cup water. Add chicken pieces and brown. Add 1 cup water and bring to boil. Add *ʻulu* and simmer for 15 minutes. Turn off heat, garnish with green onions. Makes 12, ½ cup servings. *(½ cup = 209.2 kcal., 7 gm. fat, 10.7% fat)*

'ULU WITH MUSHROOMS AND *HŌʻIʻO*

2 cups	*ʻUlu*, cooked and cubed
1 cup	Shiitake mushrooms, sliced
2 cup	*Hōʻiʻo*, sliced
½ cup	Green onions
1 cup	Chicken broth
1 oz.	*ʻŌpae*
1 cup	Water

Soak mushrooms in a bowl of hot water until soft. Remove and slice (save the mushroom water for cooking). Cut the *ʻulu* into ½-inch cubes. Cut the *hōʻiʻo* into 1" pieces, wash under cold tap water, and drain in a colander. Cut the green onions into 1" pieces. Place the mushroom water, mushrooms, and *ʻōpae* in a wok or large pan over medium to high heat and cook for 2 minutes. Stir. Add the *ʻulu*, chicken broth, and water. Cook for 5 minutes. Stir. Add green onions, stir and serve. Serve warm. Makes 5, ½ cup servings. *(½ cup = 101 kcal., 0.917 gm. fat, 8% fat)*

 **HERB 'ULU SALAD**

2 cups	*'Ulu*, cooked and cubed
1 med.	Round onion, diced
½ cup	Fresh green onions, diced
½ cup	Fresh parsley, diced
½ cup	Fat-free sour cream *or* fat-free mayonnaise
1 tsp.	Black pepper
1 tsp.	*Pa'akai*

Toss all ingredients, except sour cream, together. Add sour cream, *pa'akai*, and pepper. Mix and chill. Makes 4, ½ cup servings. *(½ cup = 129 kcal., 0.680 gm. fat, 4.7% fat)*

While living in *Hilo*, we had two large *lā'au 'ulu* which were always bearing fruit that we did not want to waste. There were always potlucks to go to and the *'Ulu* Salad recipe was created because we were so blessed with *'ulu*. It soon became a popular dish requested by friends when an occasion arrived.

 **'ULU SALAD**

3	*'Ulu*, baked or steamed and cut into bite-size pieces
1 stick	Kamaboko, diced, *or* 1 cup of cooked shrimp
1 box	Broccoli (frozen), chopped and drained
½	Round onion, diced
1 cup	Pasta
1 cup	Fat-free mayonnaise
1 tsp.	Salt
	Garlic powder to taste
	Black pepper to taste

Mix all ingredients together. Add garlic powder and pepper to taste. Chill and serve. Makes 20, ½ cup servings. *(½ cup = 71 kcal., 0.2 gm. fat, 3% fat)*

OTHER FOODS OF THE *WAI'ANAE* DIET

SEAFOOD

Ka 'Ōpelu

The *'ōpelu* and the *aku* are *malihini* to Hawaiian waters. In his migration to *Hawai'i* the great *Kahuna Pā'ao* brought these fish to *Hawai'i*. There was a battle going on between *Pā'ao* and his brother. As *Pā'ao* sailed to *Hawai'i*, his brother made the sea rough for the canoe's passage. The *'ōpelu* and the *aku* swam before the canoe to still the ocean. *Ka po'e kahiko* used to *hānai* the *'ōpelu* with the shavings of the cooked *kalo* and the *'ōpelu* in return would give themselves to *ka po'e lawai'a* when he needed to feed his family. Today there are still those who follow this tradition of *hānai*.

The *'ōpelu* and *aku* are eaten raw, boiled, baked, or *lawalu* style and are favorite for many *'ohana*.

HOW TO PREPARE *'ŌPELU*

Lightly run a spoon over the outside of the *'ōpelu* to remove the scales. Slit the *'ōpelu* from the *piko* on underside of the *'ōpū* towards the head. Remove the gills along with the intestines and leave the fish on its side. Push your thumb in between the center bone and the flesh starting from just below the head. Run your thumb downward, toward the tail, to separate the flesh from the bone and butterfly the fish. Run your index finger along the opposite side of the bone and remove bone from fish. Rub the liver and lungs of the *'ōpelu* lightly over the *'ōpelu*, then discard. This adds taste to the *'ōpelu*.

 ## Raw 'Ōpelu

Sprinkle cleaned and deboned *'ōpelu* with *pa'akai 'alaea*. Roll *'ōpelu* from the head with the flesh facing up toward the tail and place in a bowl. If you are not a "real raw fish eater" (one who eats the head also), remove the head. Chill.

The old style of eating *'ōpelu* is to open the *'ōpelu* on a dish and scrape the meat away from the skin to eat. If *lomi* style is desired, garnish with chopped *limu kohu*, chopped tomatoes, chopped green onions, and some *wai nī'oi*. Scrape and eat. Makes 1 serving.

 ## 'Ōpelu Kupa

3	*'Ōpelu*, cleaned
	Water
1 cup	Fish stock
	Green onions, chopped

Bring 3 quarts of water to a boil. Add 3 cleaned *'ōpelu* which have been cut in half. Cook approximately 10 minutes and turn off the heat. Place 1 *'ōpelu* in a saimin bowl and pour 1 cup of fish stock from the pot over the fish. Garnish with chopped green onions.

'Āweoweo Kai

A favorite fish of *Hawai'i* because of it's versatility and firm *'ono* flesh. Many families prefer to feed the *'āweoweo* to *kamali'i* or *nā kūpuna* because there are not many bones.

The *'āweoweo* would be scaled, slit, then salted on the insides overnight. The salt was then removed by rinsing. The *'āwoweo* was then cooked *pūlehu* style. After the fish was *pau*, it would be placed in a bowl, sprinkled with green onions, grated ginger and Chinese parsley (all of these are optional to taste). Enough hot water would be added to make soup stock. Every part of the fish except for the bones would be relished with the *kupa* and eaten with *poi*.

Kala

The *kala* or unicorn fish can be netted, speared, or caught with a pole. Its favorite food is the *limu lipoa*, and its flesh is fragrant with the aroma of this *limu*. You can bake, steam, or *pūlehu* the *kala* without having to clean it first. As a young child, I would watch my Auntie take the cooked flesh and dip it into the *na'au* before eating it. For years I could not bring myself to eat this fish. Today, I love to eat *pūlehu kala* with a sauce of *wai nī'oi*, a little shoyu, and lemon. If you are not used to the *na'au*, eat around!

Halalū

During the months of July through December everyone watches the beaches for the site of others with their bamboo fishing poles. Yes, it is *halalū* season! Upon seeing this we would run home, grab our bamboo poles, bait, and bucket. Sometimes it would be very crowded and people would be shoulder to shoulder, but it would be lots of fun for all ages. The school of *halalū* would swim back and forth, grabbing the bait as it went along. You would hear squeals of laughter from the *kamaliʻi* as they lifted their poles with their catch!

Halalū is the young *akule* which are about 4 to 6 inches in length. This fish can be salted and dried, pickled, broiled, or eaten raw.

Manini

A common reef fish, the name *manini* is also associated with a stingy person. *Manini* can be caught in nets or by a pole. The whole fish can be cooked *pūlehu* style and eaten with *poi, ʻuala, kalo,* or *ʻulu*. Another way is to add hot water and green onions after cooking.

Pakaliao

Codfish, not native to Hawaiian waters but introduced in its dried, salted form needing no refrigeration soon became a versatile and economic food product. It is called "bakaliao" by the Portuguese. *Pakaliao kū* is just one of the recipes adopted because it could feed large families.

In a large stew pot, boil *pakaliao*, throw away the water from the first boil and repeat. Add 1 cooked, diced *'ulu*; 2 cooked, diced *kalo*; and 3 sliced round onions; and 3 chopped carrots. Add bay leaf; garlic powder to taste and simmer on medium fire for 1 hour. Add 3 large tomatoes, cut into wedges; 3 stalks of celery, chopped; and 1 small chopped head cabbage or Portuguese cabbage. Reduce heat and let simmer for at least 1 hour.

Poke

Poke is a popular way of preparing fish today in *Hawai'i*. *Poke* (not poki) means to cut into blocks. Traditionally, *poke* was fish cut open, gutted, salted with *pa'akai*, and set aside for a couple of hours. Later it will be mixed with *'inamona, nī'oi,* and *limu*. Many other cultures have added their variations of *poke* by adding shoyu, sesame oil, sesame seeds, and green onions.

 ### POKE I'A

This is the plain style. Cut filets into 1" cubes and sprinkle with *pa'akai 'alaea*. Toss and chill.

Limu Kohu Poke

1 lb.	Fish, cubed (your choice of fish)
½ cup	*Limu kohu*
¼ cup	Green onions, chopped (optional)
	Pa'akai 'alaea to taste

Cut fish into 1" cubes and place in a bowl. Add *limu*, green onions, and *pa'akai 'alaea*. Mix and chill. Makes 8, ¼ cup servings. *(113 kcal, 6 gms. fat, 38% fat)*

Poke Shoyu Style

1 lb.	Fish, cubed (your choice of fish)
1/8 cup	Low-sodium shoyu
1 Tbsp.	Sesame seeds, mashed
¼ cup	Green onions, chopped
1 clove	Garlic, finely chopped
1 Tbsp.	*Nī'oi*, chopped (optional)
½ cup	*Limu kohu* (or what is available)

Cut fish into 1" cubes and place in a bowl. Add green onions and *limu*. In a separate bowl, mix shoyu, sesame seeds, garlic, and *nī'oi*. Stir well. Mix in fish and marinate in refrigerator for at least 1 hour prior to serving. Makes 8, ¼ cup servings. *(130 kcal, 6.6 gms. fat, 47% fat)*

May also add sliced watercress or chopped *ho'i'o* to this recipe.

Pipipi

What *kamaliʻi* has not gathered *pipipi* from the rocks on the shoreline while papa fished or mama picked *limu*. To clean the *pipipi*, we soaked it in fresh water to allow it to clean itself out. Mama would boil the *pipipi* in water, add some vegetables, and we would have an *onolicious* meal.

Pipipi Kupa

3 cups	*Pipipi*
2 large	Round onions, sliced
2 large	Tomatoes, sliced
1 quart	Water
	Paʻakai for taste

Boil water, add *pipipi*, onions, and tomatoes. Sprinkle *paʻakai* to taste. Bring to full boil. Turn heat down and simmer for 5 minutes. To serve, put soup into a bowl and have a needle available to remove meat from shell. Makes 4, 1 cup servings.

Kūpe‘e

The *kūpe‘e* is a larger version of the *pipipi* with various colors that can only be gathered at night. We would have to be very quiet for if they heard us coming they would fall off the rocks and hide in the sand. The shell of the *kūpe‘e* is highly treasured for the making of necklaces, bracelets, and anklets.

KŪPE‘E AND BLACK BEANS

2 cups	*Kūpe‘e*
1"	Ginger, peeled and grated
2 cloves	Garlic, finely chopped
¼ cup	Daucee (black beans)
¼ cup	Mirin
1 Tbsp.	Cornstarch
½ cups	Water
¼ cup	Green onions, chopped

Pre-boil *kūpe‘e*, cool off, then remove meat from shell with a needle and put on the side. Grate 2 fingers (1") of peeled ginger and 2 finely chopped cloves of garlic. Saute in pan sprayed with Pam. Heat sauce pan, add rinsed daucee and ¼ cup mirin. In a small bowl, mix together 1 tablespoon of cornstarch with ½ cup of water and add to saucepan to thicken mixture. Cook for 1 minute and immediately pour over *kūpe‘e*. Sprinkle with green onions and serve. Makes 4, ½ cup servings. *(1 serving = 220.7 kcal., 5.398 gm. fat, 22% fat)*

HŌʻONOʻONO ʻAI

The diet of *ka poʻe kahiko* was usually eaten in its natural state. Very few condiments were added to their food except *paʻakai*, *ʻalaea*, *inamona*, and *nīʻoi*. *Paʻakai* was and is still considered not only a condiment but *"iʻa"* as well. One would eat *paʻakai* alone with *poi* when times were hard. *Lau kī*, while not a condiment, adds its flavor to foods that are prepared in it. Different varieties of *limu* would also enhance the aroma and taste of prepared foods. Here you will find how to gather (or buy) and prepare some of these condiments for use with the recipes of this book.

Paʻakai

Paʻakai has been used by the *kānaka maoli* for centuries, as a preservative, as a cleansing agent, for religious purposes, and for adding flavor.

Paʻakai is composed of crystals of seawater residue that evaporate on the rocks or artificially hollowed places along the seashores of *Hawaiʻi*. It is much more abrasive than the ordinary table salt that is bought in the supermarkets.

The *kānaka maoli* gathered *paʻakai* from the shorelines and took care to keep it clean. After gathering *paʻakai* from the shorelines, it was hung in gourds or baskets. Today it is dried in rice or burlap bags.

Pa'akai gathered close to the sea, is pure white and used for seasoning foods. *Pa'akai* gathered further from the seashore, is used to preserve foods.

Today, *pa'akai* is only gathered from isolated areas on *Moloka'i* and *Kaua'i*. *Pa'akai* may be purchased from any grocery store. If you would like to gather it yourself, be sure it is from an isolated area that has not been defiled.

'Alaea

'Alaea is a red mineral deposit composed of iron oxides found mainly on *Wai'ale'ale* on *Kaua'i* and in isolated areas of *Moloka'i*, *Maui*, and *Hawai'i*.

'Alaea is used extensively in the medicinal practices of the *kānaka maoli*. It is prepared with the juices of different plants to be administered to patients with hemorrhagic problems, menstrual disorders, and to build red blood. Coincidentally, western medicine today prescribe iron supplements for similar ailments. *'Alaea* is also used to make a red paint for dye.

Today *'alaea* is still being used by traditional practitioners and as a coloring for *pa'akai*.

Pa'akai 'alaea can be purchased from most grocery stores. *'Alaea* can also be obtained on the island of *Kaua'i*. The piece must be stored in a jar or plastic bag to keep out moisture. To add *'alaea* to *pa'akai*, finely grind or grate and add to *pa'akai*. Shake jar to distribute evenly.

Kai Nī'oi

To make 2 cups of *kai nī'oi*, wash ½ cup *ni'oi*. Boil 2 cups of water. Mix together *nī'oi*, 2 cloves of garlic, boiled water, and 2 tablespoons of vinegar. Store in a clean container and refrigerate.

'Inamona

As a young girl, I was fortunate to visit my uncle at *Pu'u o Hōkū* Ranch on the island of *Moloka'i*. Our cousin would take us up to *Lanikaula*, the sacred *kukui* grove, to gather *kukui* nuts. We would always ask before entering the grove and would not be allowed to "play around." After gathering the *kukui* nuts, we would return to the ranch house and rinse the nuts. They would then be placed in a pan and put in the oven for about an hour. Newspapers would be placed on the dining table, and we would all sit around with our butter knives and bowls. One person would crack the nuts, while the rest of us would scoop out the meat. The meat would be put through a meat grinder and mixed with *pa'akai* for later use.

For a 14-ounce jar, you will need at least a gallon of *kukui* nuts. Rinse, place in a baking pan, and roast in a 350° F. oven for at least an hour or until the nuts begin to crack. Let cool, crack the nuts open, and scoop out the meat. Either place through the blender, meat grinder, or chop fine with a knife. Store in a clean jar in the refrigerator.

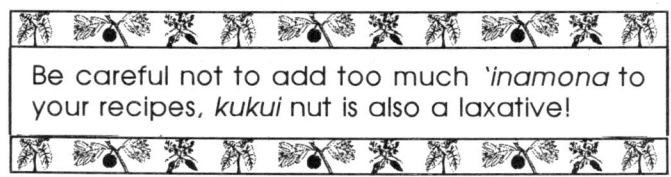

Be careful not to add too much *'inamona* to your recipes, *kukui* nut is also a laxative!

LIMU

Limu Līpoa
(much branched and brown)

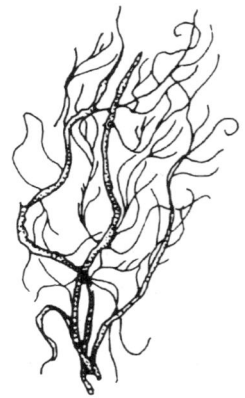

Limu 'Ele 'Ele
(long and green)

Limu Kohu
(soft, tufted, and red)

Limu Manauea *(Ogo)*
(red round branches)

Moʻolelo O Nā Limu

According to the *Kumulipo*, everything born has its place, for everything in the sea, there is a twin on the land; for all of life, there is balance. For the *limu wāwaeʻiole* there is the *wāwaeʻiole* which grows in the *uka*. For *manauea*, the succulent red seaweed, there is also a *kalo* with reddish *hāhā*. The *limu līpoa* is a highly prized, aromatic *limu* used in foods as one would use pepper. There is also the *līpoa kuahiwi*, a non-edible mountain moss.

I remember when we were young and needed to *ʻohi limu manauea* or *wāwaeʻiole* we would go down to *Ewa*. The shoreline would be full of *limu*. We would dive under the water and come up covered in *limu* to scare the smaller children. All one had to do was pick what was needed. Today, you will find not find this bounty along the shores of *Ewa*.

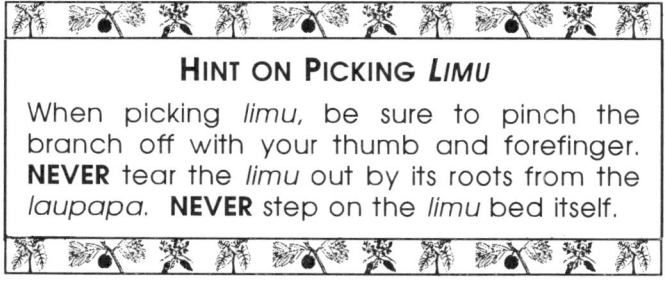

Hint on Picking *Limu*

When picking *limu*, be sure to pinch the branch off with your thumb and forefinger. **NEVER** tear the *limu* out by its roots from the *laupapa*. **NEVER** step on the *limu* bed itself.

LIMU LĪPEʻEPEʻE SALAD

1 lb.	*Limu līpeʻepeʻe*, cleaned
1 cup	Low sodium soy sauce
4 large	Tomato, diced
2 large	*Maui* onions, julienne sliced
¼ cup	Vinegar
	Nīʻoi to taste

Blanch *limu* in boiling water. Drain and rinse with cold tap water. Mix in a large bowl diced tomatoes and onions. Add soy sauce, vinegar, and *nīʻoi*; mix well. Chill and serve cold as a condiment. Makes 8, 1/8 cup servings.
(1 serving = 64 kcal., 0.164 gm. fat, 2.3% fat)

LIMU WĀWAEʻIOLE SALAD

1 lb.	*Limu wāwaeʻiole*, cleaned
1 pkg.	Cuttle fish (8 oz.), soft
4 large	Tomato, diced
2 large	*Maui* onions, julienne sliced
1 cup	Vinegar (white *or* cider)
1 Tbsp.	Sugar
3 Tbsp.	Fresh ginger, grated
	Nīʻoi, ground (if desired)

Blanch *limu* in boiling water, drain and rinse in cold tap water. Add onions, tomatoes, and cuttle fish. Mix well. Make a sauce of vinegar, sugar, ginger, and *nīʻoi*. Add sauce, mix well, cover, and chill. Makes 8, 1/8 cup servings. *(1 serving = 140 kcal., 0.964 gm. fat, 6.1% fat)*

LIMU ʻELEʻELE

Limu ʻeleʻele, rinsed and cleaned
Paʻakai to taste

After picking *limu ʻeleʻele* from shoreline waters, soak overnight in a bucket of water. The following day, remove the limu without stirring the bottom of the bucket, where much of the sand and dirt have settled. In another bucket rinse the *limu ʻeleʻele* thoroughly, washing out sand and dirt, until the water is clear. Discard any remaining *ʻōpala*. Rinse and place *limu* in clean, large bowl. Rinse and drain. Add *paʻakai* to taste and refrigerate. Use as a condiment.

FERNS

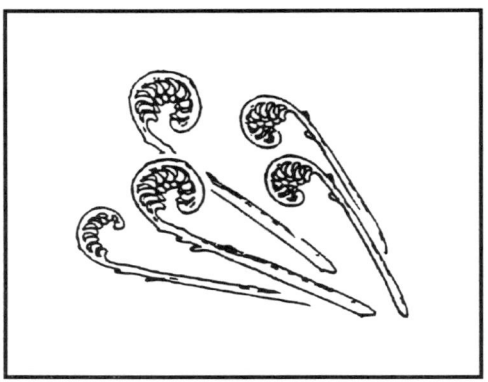

Hōʻiʻo

Hōʻiʻo grows wild in moist mountainous areas and is cultivated in the *Waipiʻo* Valley on the island of *Hawaiʻi*.

Hōʻiʻo is eaten as a vegetable or condiment. It can be eaten raw or partially cooked and is available in the supermarket under an assortment of names such as warabi (Japanese), kosade (Korean), pako (Filipino) and *pohole* on the island of *Maui*.

Preparing *Hōʻiʻo*

Hōʻiʻo is prepared by removing the tough, fibrous portion of the stem. Rinse and clean before using.

Hōʻiʻo may be chopped fine and added to *poke*. It can be added to vegetable dishes either cooked or raw.

Hōʻiʻo Salad

1 lb.	*Hōʻiʻo*
3 med.	Tomatoes, diced
2 med.	Round onions, diced
1	Lemon, halved

Soak *hōʻiʻo* for half an hour, then rinse off clean. In hot boiling water, blanch *hōʻiʻo*, for 3 minutes. Cut *hōʻiʻo* in 1 to 2 inch pieces. Put in a large bowl, add tomatoes and onions and lemon juice. Mix together and chill. Makes 6 to 8, 1 cup servings. *(1 serving = 82 kcal., 0.450 gm. fat, 4.9% fat)*

Hāpu'u

Hāpu'u is a common tree fern in *Hawai'i*, often reaching 16 feet tall. *Hāpu'u* is widely cultivated and used as an ornamental plant and a shade tree for flowers. Most of the trunk of the *hāpu'u* consists of dark interwoven root, that surrounds a central stem. The root masses make good potting soil. At the top of the trunk is a cluster of shoots. The shoots may grow 6 to 10 feet long and are divided into hundreds of small segments. These shoots are delicious when prepared properly. The young stems are covered with a brownish, silky material; this is called *pulu*. The *pulu* and green scrapings from the stem are used for medicine.

How To Prepare *Hāpuʻu* Shoots

Be sure to cut the *hāpuʻu* shoots at least 1" to 2" from the main tree. Remove the *pulu* and wash thoroughly. Cut into 3" pieces. Put the *hāpuʻu* into a pot and cover with water. Boil for approximately 30 minutes (steam from boiling water can make eyes teary). After 30 minutes, check one of the *hāpuʻu* pieces by pushing the skin. If it comes off easily, it is cooked. Cool, then peel the skin from the *hāpuʻu*. Slice into smaller pieces. Put the *hāpuʻu* in a glass gallon container, add water to cover. Change the water often for a period of 2 days or until the water is clear. Refrigerate in gallon container with the water. The *hāpuʻu* may now be used to cook and eat.

Hāpuʻu Hekka

1 lbs.	Chicken, skinless/boneless, sliced thin
2 cups	*Hāpuʻu* shoots
2 cups	Bamboo shoots, sliced thin
2 cups	Shiitake mushrooms, sliced thin
1 bunch	Watercress, sliced
1 can	Water chestnuts, sliced thin
1 bunch	Green onions, sliced thin
4 cloves	Garlic, medium size and crushed
2 cups	Shiitake water

Stir fry chicken in a hot wok sprayed with Pam. Add garlic. Soak shiitake mushrooms in 2 cups of water, then slice. Add bamboo shoots and sliced shiitake mushrooms. Add water chestnuts, *hāpuʻu* shoots, and watercress. Stir fry for 5 minutes, cover with lid, and turn off. The heat

(continued next page)

from the wok will continue the cooking process and vegetables will be crunchy. Makes 12, 1 cup servings.
(1 cup = 162 kcal., 6 gm. fat, 33.3% fat)

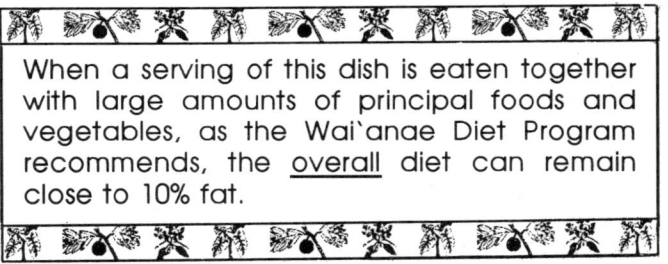

When a serving of this dish is eaten together with large amounts of principal foods and vegetables, as the Wai`anae Diet Program recommends, the <u>overall</u> diet can remain close to 10% fat.

FRUITS USED ON THE *WAI‘ANAE* DIET

Although *Hawai‘i* is known as tropical islands with luscious fruits, there are, in reality, very few indigenous fruits. The precious *‘ohelo* is probably the only native. The *mai‘a* was introduced by the *kānaka maoli*, and all other fruits have been introduced through the years. Fruits used on the *Wai‘anae* Diet are usually served in their natural state.

Mai'a

Mai'a is a well known fruit throughout the world. *Ka Po'e Kahiko* brought the *mai'a* plants with them when they migrated to *Hawai'i*. Most of the *mai'a* were of the cooking variety. Women were not allowed to eat certain varieties until the eating *kapu* was broken.

Ma'ia is eaten raw or cooked, depending on the variety being used. The leaves are used in the *imu*, as well as to wrap the bodies of the *ali'i*. Stumps were used for target practice in spear throwing. The sap from the flower is used as medicine. Many still believe it to be bad luck to take *mai'a* out to sea when fishing.

'Alani

The *'alani* was introduced to *Hawai'i* in 1792, by a Captain George Vancouver. *'Alani* was the first fruit to be cultivated commercially and, at one time the, leading export from *Kona*. *Waialua*, *O'ahu*, and *Waimea*, *Kaua'i* also have their varieties of oranges.

Mīkana

The *mīkana* is believed to have been introduced to *Hawai'i* in 1823 from the Marquesas islands. In 1919, the solo variety was introduced by the *Hawai'i* Agricultural Experiment Station (CES) and has become an important export.

Hala Kahiki

The *hala kahiki* is a native of South America and is believed to have been brought to *Hawai'i* by a Spaniard in 1813. *Hala kahiki* was first planted on the island of *Hawai'i*, in the gardens of the visitors. Once an important export, it now gives way to "progress."

FROZEN *MAI'A* DESSERT

4 med.   *Mai'a*, ripe and frozen

Place in a blender frozen *mai'a* and process through. Put in ½ cup containers and serve. Makes 8 servings.
(½ = 118 kcal., 0.341 gm fat, 2.6% fat)

MIXED FRUIT SALAD

1 med.	*Mīkana*, cubed
3	*'Alini*, cubed
4	*Mai'a*, sliced
2 cups	Fat-free yogurt

Toss fruits together in a bowl and mix in yogurt. Chill. Makes 8, ½ cup servings. *(½ cup = 124.7 kcal., 0.250 gm. fat, 1.8% fat)*

OTHER FRUITS OF *HAWAI‘I*

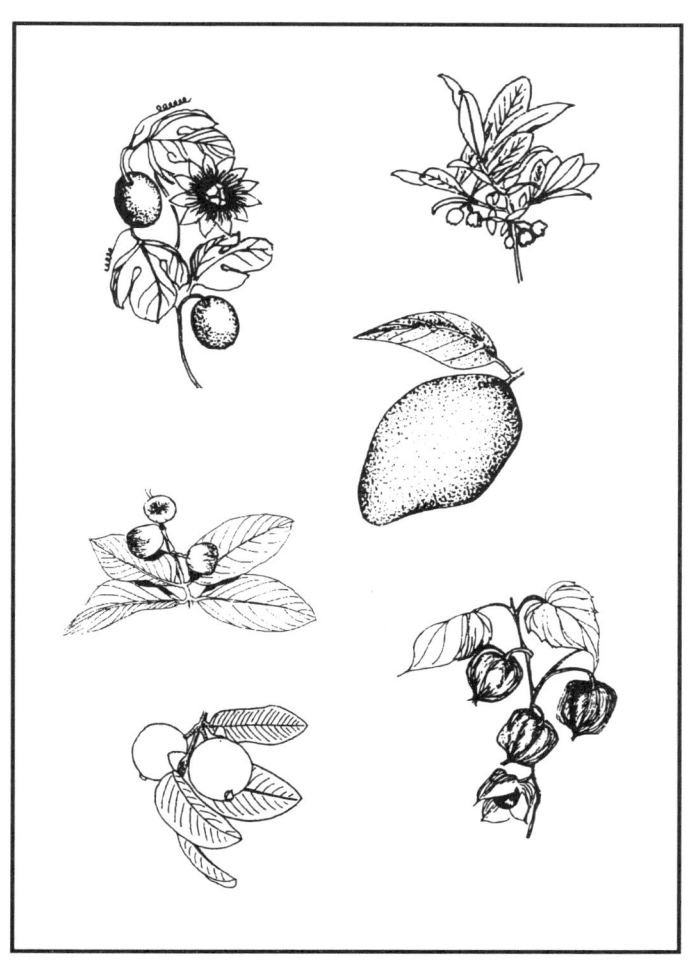

'Ōhelo Berries

A native shrub, *'Ōhelo* berries are sacred to *Pele*. It grows in the volcanic soil of the islands of *Hawai'i* and *Maui*. Of the cranberry family, it bears red or yellow berries. The berries can be eaten raw, but is most often used to make sauces, jellies, and pastries. The leaves may be brewed into a tea.

Kuawa

Now the most common wild fruit in *Hawai'i*, it was brought from Australia to be cultivated. Its fruits are edible raw, but commonly made into jellies, jam, juices, and sherbets. The leaves have medicinal properties and can be made into tea.

Manakō

The *manakō*, plentiful in *Hawai'i*, is native to Asia and was introduced to *Hawai'i* in the early 1800's. Eaten green or ripe, *manako* has always been a favorite of young and old. They say you are old when you use a knife to cut into a ripe *manakō*, for only the *kamali'i* will tear away the skin with their teeth and eat it on the spot.

'Ōhi'a 'Ai

Brought to *Hawai'i* by early Polynesians, the mountain apple is native to the Malayan Archipelago. It's fruits can be eaten and the bark is used for medicinal purposes.

Liliko'i

The *liliko'i*, an American vine with yellow or purple fruits, grows wild in the forests of *Hawai'i*. Jams, jellies, juices, and pastries are made from this fruit.

Pohā

Introduced to *Hawai'i*, *pohā* is cultivated and grows wild. It has tart-like berries which are made into jams and sherbets.

Fruit Relish

1 cup	*Pohā* berries, chopped
1 cup	*'Ōhelo* berries, chopped
1 cup	*Manako*, ripe and chopped
¼ cup	Brown sugar

Mix together. Can be used as a jam or glaze on baked fish or chicken. Makes 12, ¼ cup servings. *(43 kcal., 0.42 gm. fat, 0.08% fat)*

Cook ingredients over a slow fire and use as a glaze over 'uala or 'ulu for a wonderful dessert.

Wai Hua

1 cup	*Pohā* berries, chopped
1 cup	*'Ōhelo* berries, chopped
1 cup	Lemon juice
	Sugar substitute, to taste
	Mint leaves
	Lime, sliced

Blend together in juicer. Add 2 quarts of water, sugar substitute to taste, mint leaves and lime wheels. Service ice cold. Makes 2 servings. *(90 kcal., 0.5 gm. fat, 0.5% fat)*

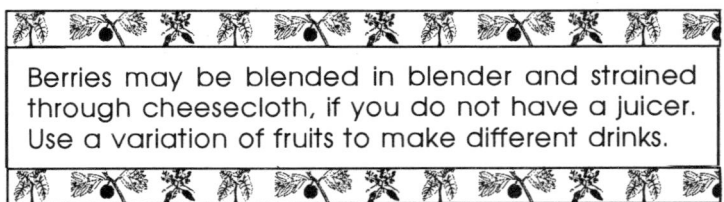

Berries may be blended in blender and strained through cheesecloth, if you do not have a juicer. Use a variation of fruits to make different drinks.

MANAKO SMOOTHIE

2   *Manako*, ripe, peeled, sliced, and frozen

Place frozen *manako* in a blender and process. Put into ½ cup container and serve. Makes 3 to 4, ½ cup servings.
(104 kcal., 0.75 gm. fat, 0.06% fat)

'ŌHELO 'ALANI JAM

2 cups	*'Ōhelo* berries, fresh and finely chopped
1 Tbsp.	*'Alani* rind, grated
1 med.	*'Alani*, peeled, seeded, and chopped fine
¼ tsp.	Ginger, ground
¼ tsp.	Nutmeg, ground

Mix and keep refrigerated. Makes 32, 1 teaspoon servings.
(1 teaspoon = 6 kcal., 0.03 gm. fat, 0.04% fat)

HAWAIIAN HERB TEAS

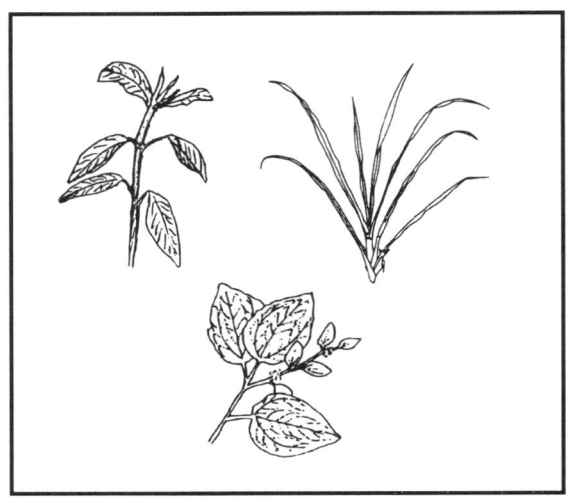

Koʻokoʻolau

Koʻokoʻolau is a many branched native shrub that may grow up to three feet high. It can be found on the outskirts of the forest. It is a plant with woody stems that support slender green branches, each with three to five pairs of leaves. The leaves are oval-shaped with pointed tips on stems half as long as the leaf. *koʻokoʻolau* has a yellowish flower that give way to narrow, barbed seeds. Sometimes the *Nehe* or Spanish needle is mistaken for *koʻokoʻolau*. This imported weed grows wild everywhere in *Hawaiʻi* and can be used for a tea named *kinehe*.

Koʻokoʻolau is used both as a tea and as a medicine by the *kānaka maoli*. *Kinehe* is used only as a tea.

Wāpine

Wāpine is an oil grass that originated from southern Asia. When this grass is cut or crushed, the leaves release a lemon essence. *Wāpine* grows in tufts, with green pointed leaves or blades two to three feet long with fine saw-toothed edges.  *Wāpine* is used as a tea, for cooking, and as a medicine by the Hawaiians.

Mamaki

 *Mamaki* is a shrub or a small- to medium-size tree that may grow up to 30 feet tall. It is usually found on the outskirts of forests and in clearings. The *mamaki* has toothed leaves that are white beneath with veins on the lower surface that may be green, reddish, or purplish.

The *kānaka maoli* of today is still using the *mamaki* leaves as a tea and for medicine as did *ka poʻe kahiko*.

Hot Tea

There are several ways to make tea. Bring 4 cups of water to a boil and add dried leaves.

For *mamaki* tea, 1 medium-sized leaf will go a long way. the longer the leaf is left in, the stronger the brew will be.

Ko'oko'olau leaves are smaller so 4 leaves may be required to make a tea of the same amount.

For *wāpine* tea, use 4 long stalks which have been cut.

Experiment with the amounts to suit your individual taste.

ICED TEA

On a hot day, add ice, mint leaves, pineapple wedges, and lemon or lime wheels to *ko'oko'olau* or *mamaki* tea.

GLOSSARY

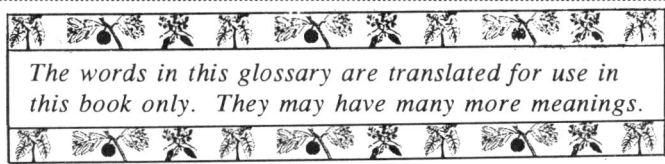

The words in this glossary are translated for use in this book only. They may have many more meanings.

Aku – Bonito or skipjack tuna. A fond fish of *Hawai'i* for every part can be eaten either raw or cooked. Also used by fishermen as a lure in marlin fishing. This fish is *malihini* to *Hawai'i*. It traveled with the *Kahuna Pā'ao* along with the *'ōpelu* and calmed the seas in front of his canoe. Also thought of as an *'aumakua* by some *kanaka maoli*.

Akule – Big-eyed or goggle-eyed scad fish.

'Alaea – Water soluble, colloidal ocherous earth used for coloring salt, as medicine, dye for *kapa*, or in purification ceremonies.

'Alani – The orange fruit or the color orange.

Ali'i – Chief, chiefess, royalty. There were many different levels of *ali'i*. See Mary Kawena Pukui, Samuel H. Ebert's <u>Hawaiian Dictionary</u>.

'Aumakua, 'Aumākua *(pl)* – Family or personal gods; deified ancestors who might assume the shape of sharks, owls, hawks, rocks, plants, or forms that would aid a

71

family member. A symbiotic relationship existed between mortals and their 'aumākua. The forms of 'aumākua were not harmed or eaten; and 'aumākua warned and reprimanded mortals in dreams, visions, and calls.

'Awa – A plant also known as kava, native to the Pacific. It is used to make a narcotic drink for medicinal and spiritual purposes.

'Āweoweo – Various species of red fishes, sometimes called bigeye. Much desired for feeding young children and the elderly because it has little bone.

Daucee – Fermented black beans, used mainly in Chinese cooking.

Enenue – Also known as *nenue* or *manaloa*, the chub, rudder, or pilot fish. A much desired fish because of the strong *limu* aroma of its flesh, it is usually eaten raw.

Hāhā – The stem of the *kalo* plant used in cooking. The outer part of the stem must be removed before cooking, and *hāhā* should never be eaten raw.

Hala Kahiki – Pineapple, an introduced fruit to *Hawai'i*, turned into a large industry which is now declining.

Halalū – Young of the *akule*.

Hāloa – Far reaching, long stemmed. Second born child of *Wākea* and *Papa*.

Hāloanaka – First born child of *Wākea* and *Papa*.

Hānai – Foster or adopted child. To raise feed, nourish, caretaker; this term was used affectionately for a chief who cared for his subjects. While the custom of *"hānai"* was much exercised in *Hawai'i*, a child was never spoken of as "the one we adopted." All children brought into a household were loved equally.

Hāpu'u – Once a common tree fern and cultivated, it, too, must be protected before it becomes extinct along with the forest of *Hawai'i*. The *pulu* or soft brown hairs on the outside of the trunk were once harvested to stuff mattresses and pillows. The *pulu* was also used to stuff corpses. The young center shoot can be cooked and tastes much like bamboo shoots.

He'e – Octopus, mistakenly called squid. Literally meaning to "flee," *he'e* was often given to the sick so that the ailment would flee or leave.

Heiau – Place of worship for *kanaka maoli*; many different types.

Hekka – Japanese word for mixed vegetables. A term used in cooking, such as chicken hekka – a dish of stir-fried chicken with mixed vegetables.

Hō'i'o – A native fern. Young fronds are eaten raw. Orientals call this fern "warabi" and use it in cooking.

Hō'ono'ono 'Ai – To make tasty, flavor. Condiment, relish.

Hula – A dance, song, or chant.

Humuhumunukunukuapua'a – The state fish. See page 25.

I'a – Fish or any marine animal. Meat or any flesh food, such as *pipi i'a* (beef). Any food eaten as a relish with *poi*, *'uala*, *'ulu*, or *kalo*.

Imu – Underground earth oven.

'Inamona – Relish made of the kernel of *kukui*, mashed with salt.

Kahe – Strip or cut diagonally lengthwise.

Kai – Sea or sea water.

Kai nī'oi – Chili pepper water.

Kala – A common reef fish, also known as the unicorn fish.

Kalo – Taro, the staff of life, main staple of the *kanaka maoli*. Usually associated with the corm of the *kalo* plant.

Kamaboko – Japanese word for a type of fish cake, usually colored pink. It also comes in green and yellow during the Christmas holidays.

Kamali'i – Children, used when speaking of more than one child of mixed sexes.

Kamapu'a – A demigod associated with the god *Lono*. Appears in many mythological tales throughout the islands.

Kanaka Maoli, Kānaka Maoli *(pl)* – In Mary K. Pukui, Samuel H. Ebert's Hawaiian Dictionary, this term is used to identify a full-blooded Hawaiian person. Today, this term is used for all those of original native descent from *Hawaiʻi*. The word *"kanaka"* means human being, man, person. The word *"maoli"* means native, indigenous, genuine. The term *"kānaka maoli"* speaks of the indigenous people of *Hawaiʻi*. The term "Hawaiian" is English and not what the *"kānaka maoli"* call themselves.

Ka Pae ʻĀina – The true name for the islands of *Hawaiʻi*. (*ka/ke* - the, *pae* - cluster, group of, *ʻāina* - land, earth)

Ka poʻe Hawaiʻi – The native people of *Hawaiʻi*.

Ka poʻe kāhiko – "The people of old," spoken with much respect and fondness. (*poʻe* - people or persons, *kāhiko* - old, ancient, antique, long ago)

Kapu (eating) – Taboo, sacredness, prohibition, forbidden

Kauaʻi – Island and county of *Hawaiʻi* found at the top of the island chain.

Keiki – Child, offspring, boy, youngster; shoot or sucker as that of the *kalo* plant.

Keiki kāne – Male child.

Kinehe or Nehe – The Spanish needle plant, similar to *koʻokoʻolau*. *Kinehe* usually refers to the tea made from the leaves of the *kinehe*.

Kino lau – The many forms taken by a supernatural such as *Pele*.

Kona – Area on the island of *Hawai'i*. The leeward side of all islands.

Ko'oko'olau – A native shrub though some varieties have been introduced to *Hawai'i*, the *kanaka maoli* use the leaves to make into tea and as medicine.

Kū – The god *Kū*, also known as *Kūka'ilimoku*, *Kamehameha's* famous war god. Note: *Kū*, *Kāne*, *Kanaloa*, and *Lono* had many names – usually another name added to the main name to address that certain sphere or realm that was being governed. For example: *Kūka'ilimoku*, *Lonomakahiki*, and *Kānekawaiola*.

Kū – Used with another term such as *pipi* (cow). *Pipi kū* is beef stew. *Mo'a kū* is chicken stew, to stew.

Kuawa – Guava. A low tree, the *kuava* is native to tropical America and the most common wild fruit in *Hawai'i* today. It bears edible fruit the size of lemons. These fruits are commonly made into juice, jams, jellies, and pastries. The leaves have medicinal purposes, and the wood is used for woodworking and fire. It is believed that *kuava* was brought to *Hawai'i* from Australia and was being cultivated in the 14th century.

Kukui – Candlenut tree, the state tree. Everything from this tree was used (see Mary Kawena Pukui, Samuel H. Elbert's <u>Hawaiian Dictionary</u>). *'Inamona* was made from the nuts of this tree.

Kumulipo – The creation chant of *ka pae 'āina*, "*Hawai'i*."

Kupa – Soup, stew; boiled such as *'ōpelu kupa*, boiled *'ōpelu*.

Kūpeʻe – An edible marine snail, much like *pipipi* but larger. Valued as a food and for making jewelry such as bracelets, anklets, and necklaces. These were also called *kūpeʻe*.

Lāʻī – Or *lau kī*, the ti leaf has many uses. It is used to wrap food such as with *lawalu*. It can be made into a type of bag which can hold a *lei*, clothing, etc. *Lāʻī* can also be used for medicinal purposes or in spiritual ceremonies. You will not find a *kanaka maoli* who does not plant *lāʻī* in the yard around the home.

Lanikaula – Sacred *kukui* grove on the island of *Molokaʻi*.

Lau Kalo – The leaf of the *kalo* plant. Used in preparing many dishes, an especially favorite food of *Pele*, the volcano goddess of *Hawaiʻi*.

Lapaʻau – To heal with medicine, to practice medicine.

Laupapa – A broad flat reef, as of coral, lava, reef.

Lau ʻUala – Sweet potato leaves.

Lawaiʻa – Fisherman; fishing technique; to fish.

Lawalu – A bundle of food, usually fish which has been wrapped in *lau kalo* then *lāʻī* and steamed.

Lilikoʻi – Passion fruit. An edible American vine growing wild in the forests of *Hawaiʻi*. *Lilikoʻi* is made into juice, jams, jellies, and pastries.

Limu Eleʻele – A long, green, edible seaweed used in raw fish dishes or alone as a relish.

Limu Kohu – Much prized for its flavor, by itself, or as a relish with *poke*. The seaweed is reddish brown or purplish in color and also called *līpehe*, *līpehu*, and *līpaʻakai*.

Limu Līpeʻepeʻe – An edible, red seaweed used in raw fish dishes or as a salad is also called *līpepe*.

Limu Līpoa – A highly prized, aromatic seaweed which is used in foods as one would use pepper. There is also a *līpoa kuahiwi*, a non-edible mountain moss.

Limu Manauwea or Limu Manuaea – A small, red seaweed used for mixing with fish or as a salad. Called "ogo" by the Japanese. *Manauwea* is also the name of a type of *kalo*.

Limu Wāwaeʻiole – A spongy, green seaweed also called rat's feet by some. Used in raw fish dishes. There is also a *wāwaeʻiole* which grows inland and is used to make Christmas wreaths and *haku lei*.

Loʻi – Irrigated terrace, especially for *kalo*, but also for rice.

Lōkahi – Unity, harmony.

Lomi (style) – To rub, press, crush, massage, rub out; to work in and out.

Lūʻau – Cooked *lau kalo*, usually the *lau kalo* which has been boiled in water to cook and added to cooked *heʻe* or *moʻa*.

Maiʻa – Banana. There were many different varieties of *maiʻa* grown in *Hawaiʻi*. *Maiʻa* was one of the foods *kapu* to women in *Hawaiʻi* because it was a form of the god *Kū*, the god of war for men.

Malihini – Stranger, foreigner, newcomer, tourist; one unfamiliar with a place or custom.

Mamaki – A small, native tree whose bark is used to make *kapa* and the leaves are used for teas.

Manakō – Mango. A large tree that bears edible fruit.

Manini – Common reef fish, small striped sturgeon fish, also known as convict tang. The name is also used as a slang when implying a person is stingy or to something small.

Mīkana – Papaya, a small tree, popular in *Hawai'i* for its fruit.

Moi – Threadfish. A fish much esteemed for food. If seen in large schools, it was taken as an omen of disaster for chiefs. Also a type of *kalo*.

Mo'a – Chicken.

Mo'olelo – Story, tale, myth, history, tradition, literature, legend. All stories were oral not written.

Mo'olelo Li'ili'i – A little tale (*mo'olelo* - story, tale, myth, *li'ili'i*)

Naka – To quiver, shake, shiver, unsteady.

Na'au – Intestines, guts.

Nā Kūpuna – the elders.

Nā Wāhine – More than one woman – "the women."

Nī‘oi – Chili pepper.

Niu – Coconut.

‘Oha – The corm or bulb root of the *kalo* plant. See page 11 for picture.

Ohana – Family, relative, kin group; related.

‘Ōhelo – A small, native shrub similar to cranberries. The fruit is sacred to *Pele*, to whom offerings were made. It is an edible fruit which can be used to make jams, pastries, and juices.

‘Ohi – To gather, harvest.

‘Ōhi‘a ‘Ai – The mountain apple, whose fruits can be eaten and the bark used for medicinal purposes.

Ō‘ī‘o – Ladyfish or bonefish. This fish is eaten either raw mixed with *limu kohu* or used to make fish cake, which is steamed.

‘Ono – Delicious, tasty, savory; to relish, crave; deliciousness, flavor, savor.

‘Onolicious – A slang word used by locals when describing a favorite food.

‘Ōpae – General name for shrimp.

‘Ōpala – Rubbish, trash, waste matter.

'Ōpelu – Mackerel scad. This fish can be eaten raw or cooked and is also used by fishermen as live bait. The *'ōpelu*, also a *malihini* to *Hawai'i*, is said to have come over to *Hawai'i* with the *Kahuna Pa'ao*. The school of *'ōpelu* were said to have calmed the seas for *Pa'ao* when they became rough. *'Ōpelu* are still thought of as an *'aumakua* by the *kanaka maoli*.

'Opū – Belly, stomach, abdomen, tripe.

Pa'akai – Sea salt. The *kanaka maoli* used to have salt farms in which pools with salt water were dried and the salt collected. The crust from tide pools is also collected and kept in bags to use.

Pa'i'ai – Cooked *kalo*, which has been mashed into a paste, form of *kalo* before it has had water added to it to make *poi*. This form could be kept longer in calabash containers, was especially used for travel.

Pa'i'ai Wai'ū – Unmixed *poi* eaten as cereal with milk.

Pakaliao – Codfish, called "bakaliao" by the Portuguese.

Pakaliao Kū – Codfish stew.

Papa – Wife of *Wākea*, mother of *Hāloa* and *Hāloanaka*.

Papa ku'i 'ai – Board used for the pounding of *poi*.

Pau – Done, finished.

Pele – Goddess of the volcano, *'aumakua* to some *kānaka maoli*.

Piko – Belly button, navel.

Pipipi – General name for small mollusks. Eaten boiled, the shells were made into jewelry.

Pō – Night, darkness; the realm of the gods.

Poʻe Lawaiʻa – Fishermen.

Pohā – Otherwise known as the cape gooseberry, *Pohā* was introduced into *Hawaiʻi*. The fruit can be eaten raw or made into jam.

Pōhaku – Rock, stone, mineral.

Pōhaku kuʻi ʻai – *Poi* pounders were made and shaped out of special *pōkahu*.

Pohale – Another name for *hoʻiʻo*, mountain fern, used on the island of *Maui*.

Poi – Cooked *kalo* which has been mashed into a paste and water has been added to it to the desired consistency. Main staple food for *kanaka maoli*.

Poke – To slice, cut crosswise into pieces, as with fish.

Pua Kalo – *Kalo* flower.

Puka – Entrance, hole, door.

Pūlehu – To broil, as *ʻuala*, *ʻulu*, or *maiʻa* on hot embers.

Pulu – The soft, glossy wool on the base of *hapuʻu*.

Shiitake – A dried mushroom, usually found in the Asian section of the grocery store or fresh in some produce departments. The dried form must be soaked in hot water for at least 10 minutes to soften. The water from soaking is usually used in recipes also.

'Uala – Sweet potato was another important staple of the *kanaka maoli*. Both the tubers and the leaves of the vine were eaten. This staple was a form of *Lono*, the god of agriculture, also associated with the demigod *Kamapua'a*. (See *Mo'olelo O 'Uala* on page 25.)

Uka – Inland, uplands toward the mountains, shore, and if at sea.

'Ulu – Breadfruit, a tree brought into *Hawai'i*. Its fruit is eaten either baked, boiled, or steamed as a starch and can be made into *poi*. The trunk was often used to make *pahu* drums, *poi* boards, and woodwork. The sap was used as a glue in the making of canoes.

Wahine – Woman, lady, wife, female relative.

Wai'ale'ale, Kaua'i – Highest mountain on the island of *Kaua'i* which has an annual rainfall of 476 inches. Literally: rippling or overflowing water.

Waialua, O'ahu – A land division of *O'ahu*.

Wai'anae – An area on the leeward side of *O'ahu* known for its good fishing grounds. Literally: mullet water.

Wai hua – Fruit juice (*wai* - water, *hua* - fruit)

Waimea, Kaua'i – Area on *Kaua'i* where Captain Cook first landed.

Wai niu – Coconut milk or water.

Waipiʻo (Valley), Hawaiʻi – Valley in north *Hawaiʻi*. Literally: curved water.

Waiʻū – Milk.

Wākea – Father of *Hāloa*.

Wāpine – Lemon grass was introduced to *Hawaiʻi*. While the leaves are used for tea, the root is also used in cooking which gives off a ginger-like flavor. Also used to make *lei*.

References for this glossary:

Mary Kawena Pukui, Samuel H. Elbert, <u>Hawaiian Dictionary</u>, 1986, 1992, University of Hawaii Press.

Mary Kawena Pukui, Samuel H. Elbert, and Esther T. Mookini, 1974, <u>Place Names of Hawaii</u>.

Notes

Notes

Notes

Notes

Notes

Notes

Notes

Notes

Other Books Available

The Wai'anae Book of Hawaiian Health

The Wai'anae Diet Program has demonstrated:
- Average weight loss in 21 days was 17.1 lbs.
- Cholesterol decreased 14%
- Blood Pressure decreased 10%
- Improved control of blood sugar

Wai'anae Diet Cookbook

Companion volume to the Wai'anae Book of Hawaiian Health. In this book you will find:
- Recipes used during the Wai'anae Diet Program
- Substitute recipes using other ethnic foods
- Recipes contributed by past participants

To order, fill out the form below:

Quantity	Title	Cost	Total Cost
	The Wai'anae Book of Hawaiian Health *The Wai'anae Diet Program Manual*	$9.95	$
	Wai'anae Diet Cookbook	$7.25	
	Wai'anae Diet Cookbook *'Elua*	$10.00	
	Eat More, Weigh Less!™ Diet Book	$13.95	
	Shipping and Handling per Book	$ 2.00	
	TOTAL		$

Send check or money order to:

Wai'anae Diet Program, Waianae Coast Comprehensive Health Center, 86-260 Farrington Highway, Wai'anae, Hawai'i 96792-3199

Name _____

Address _____

_____

City/State/Zip _____

(All proceeds support the Wai'anae Diet Program)